The Resurrection of Villiers de l'Isle-Adam

LÉON BLOY

Translated By Richard Robinson

Sunny Lou Publishing Company
Portland, Oregon, USA
http://www.sunnyloupublishing.com

1st Edition, Corrected: October 6, 2025
Original Publication Date: March 8, 2022

ISBN: 978-1-955392-24-2

* * *

This translation from French is based on
the Librairie E. Lecampion, A. Blaizot, Éditeur edition of *Le
Resurrection de Villiers de l'Isle-Adam*, Paris, 1906.

Contents

Foreword

Sed ut perspiciatis, unde omnis iste natus error sit voluptatem accusantium doloremque laudantium, totam rem aperiam eaque ipsa, quae ab illo inventore veritatis et quasi architecto beatae vitae dicta sunt, explicabo. Nemo enim ipsam voluptatem, quia voluptas sit, aspernatur aut odit aut fugit, sed quia consequuntur magni dolores eos, qui ratione voluptatem sequi nesciunt, neque porro quisquam est, qui dolorem ipsum, quia dolor sit, amet, consectetur, adipisci velit, sed quia non numquam eius modi tempora incidunt, ut labore et dolore magnam aliquam quaerat voluptatem. Ut enim ad minima veniam, quis nostrum exercitationemullam corporis suscipit laboriosam, nisi ut aliquid ex ea commodi consequatur? Quis autem vel eum iure reprehenderit, qui in ea voluptate velit esse, quam nihil molestiae consequatur, vel illum, qui dolorem eum fugiat, quo voluptas nulla pariatur? [33] At vero eos et accusamus et iusto odio dignissimos ducimus, qui blanditiis praesentium voluptatum deleniti atque corrupti, quos dolores et quas molestias excepturi sint, obcaecati cupiditate non provident, similique sunt in culpa, qui officia deserunt mollitia animi, id est laborum et dolorum fuga. Et harum quidem rerum facilis est et expedita distinctio. Nam libero tempore, cum soluta nobis est eligendi optio, cumque nihil impedit, quo minus id, quod maxime placeat, facere possimus, omnis voluptas assumenda est, omnis dolor repellendus. Temporibus autem quibusdam et aut officiis debitis aut rerum necessitatibus saepe eveniet, ut et voluptates repudiandae sint et molestiae non recusandae. Itaque earum rerum hic tenetur a sapiente delectus, ut aut reiciendis voluptatibus maiores alias consequatur aut perferendis doloribus asperiores repellat.

      – Cicero, 45 BC (*de Finibus Bonorum et Malorum*)

Invitation to Subscribers

THE SUBSCRIBERS TO FRÉDÉRIC BROU'S MONUMENT IN MEMORY OF VILLIERS DE L'ISLE-ADAM ARE INVITED TO SEND THE TOTAL AMOUNT OF THEIR SUBSCRIPTIONS TO M. A. BLAIZOT, BOOKSELLER, 22, RUE LE PELETIER, TREASURER OF THE COMMITTEE FORMED FOR THE ERECTION, IN PARIS, OF THAT EXTRAORDINARY MONUMENT.

The Resurrection of
Villiers de l'Isle-Adam

hristians do not believe in death. "*Vita mutatur, non tollitur*," so goes the Liturgy: "Life changes, it is not taken away.

If anyone had wanted that, it was poor Villiers de l'Isle-Adam. Death without return, stinking and inconceivable, such as "swan slayers" desire it, was not within him.

Here then is what happens to him all of a sudden, seventeen years after he has gone to sleep. Glory arrives, totally naked glory, without wings or aureole, the glory of miserable wretches. She pulls him out of his tomb and, setting the coffin upright, pulls off the planks with an irresistible hand... The poor, great poet who is not dead, as nothing can die, half opens his eyes like a half-wakened criminal might who asks himself whether it is the hour of his judgment or the hour of his torture.

Miserable and glorious man! He wrote several proud phrases that his contemporaries did not understand and which perhaps will thrill, in a few years, the rare survivors of Intellectuality. His departure made a great number of them rejoice: *In Nativitate ejus multi gavisi sunt*,[1] and his return will exasperate crocodiles. For he will return, I tell you, verily.

*
* *

---

[1]*In Nativitate*...: Latin for "Many rejoiced in his birth." See Luke 1:14.

Poor Villiers! I will not forget his sad funeral at Saint-François-Xavier[2] and the filthy procession of men of the quill under a torrential rain!

Of all his contemporaries whom he despised the most, a dirty bastard of a pontiff was supposed to deliver I believe the filth of a harangue over his tomb. I hightailed it halfway through.

But what a lamentable end! I have recounted it elsewhere, and it is better to give it a rest. There is enough sadness and horror in that story to lead one to an early grave...

---

[2]Saint-François-Xavier: a Roman Catholic church in the 7th arrondissement of Paris.

 belong," he said, "to the race of Beings who bring honor to men." He never wanted anyone to speak to him about another

"fatherland than exile," and life, consequently, was marvelously a bitch for that poor, sublime child.

"Every man is an addition to his race." Thus is condensed, like a bronze blade, by the Philosopher Blanc de Saint-Bonnet, all the experience of the centuries.

Which is another way of saying that from the extremity of the last branch of a great tree, singled out by lightning, forever hangs a delectable or terrifying fruit in which the precious essence makes an appearance before vanishing forever.

When it has to do with a very glorious sap, as in the case of Villiers, the grievous human being charged with assuming everything is not merely the sole bearer of splendors or miseries, divine joys or profound mournings, abasements or triumphs accumulated by so many of his ancestors. He must also bear the *Dream* of all that, bear it across the long, interminable desert, "from the uterus to the tomb," without a single soul capable of assisting him or consoling him.

He must submit to the miraculous and redoubtable heritage of a tumultuous bosom filled with all the sighs of the generations whose very name causes agony.

*
* *

The destiny of the author of *Axel* was so extraordinary that his life appeared like a foreshortening of the very history of the proud Race that he was the supreme incarnation of. Perhaps an analogy will help me explain this.

You remember perhaps those chronological abridgments that pedagogues of unappeased maledictions inflicted on our childhood? Each historical epoch is condemned to living and breathing within the space of four narrow pages, in those suffocating opuscules where the most distant and distinct events are piled one on top of the other and pressed together like salted meat in a barrel for export.

Charlemagne commingles with Merovech, the first Valois make a mastic with the Valois d'Orleans or the Valois d'Angoulême, Henry III busts the rib cage of Charles the Wise, François I is flattened under Louis the Fat, Ravaillac assasinates John the Fearless, and it is at Varennes that Louis XIV seems to sign the revocation of the Edict of Nantes. Etc. Any retreat is impossible, and it is hard to see through the chaos.

Villiers de l'Isle-Adam, last of that name, and having nothing before his eyes anymore but the growing Churlishness of the end of the last century, was himself, in some ways, one of those terrible abridgments.

Incapable of adjusting to contemporary life

which filled him with disgust, he resided deep within his own heart like a dragon in its cave before the Deluge, inconsolable and distraught because of the destruction of its species.

He truly bore the souls of all the great men of his Family within himself, and the list of them was long. He confabulated with their shadows, not disrespectfully seeking to disentangle them, but quite the opposite, and he ended up happy finally in the discovery of not knowing, in all fairness, what became of them all.

*
* *

He was, moreover, as I have already said, one of those rare adepts who deny death, persuading himself that self-preservation is a simple act of the will and that it is incomparably easier to eternalize oneself than to come to an end.

According to Villiers, the death spoken about by so many imbeciles was nothing more than an imposture, an insupportable imposture invented by fabricators of funeral wreaths and workers in marble.

He had even written, for his own personal use, a fantasy – Hegelian, alas! – on that subject, in view of establishing that beings and things have no other need for their maintenance before Infinity than what it pleases our consciences to grant.

He lived, then, amidst a proud group of people whom he had, for the longest time, obtained the resurrection of – unphased by bringing warriors or magistrates together who had been separated over the centuries and whose very personalities were lost to him in the admirable crowd of members of his family.

is journey in this world is said to be known. A marvelous legend has been made of it, even though the bizarre circumstances that some people's imagination and his own even have surcharged it with are much rarer than one might suppose.

The famous turmoil in his mind was, fundamentally, nothing but the turmoil in his soul, and it was, in that sense, really rather tragic.

I would like to say that his life was found in conformance with the very History of his Race and that that was precisely the source of his inexpressible sorrows. But how to express such a thing so that people might understand it?

This history which is right at the heart of universal History and which one learns so poorly at school was completely alive and contemporary in him. It burned him, it devoured him, like a furious flame that he was the last aliment of.

In the ardor of his tortures, his least gesture straightway reclaimed the ancient *gestures* of his Lineage in their entirety, which died standing in the ventricles of his heart.

Very few people understood him, and those who did, what could they do for so grandiose a miserable wretch? God himself, the God Moloch, unwilling to support the aristocracy any longer, demanded his holocaust.

Literary genius was given to him in spades, but that was the least part of his torture...

*
* *

How sweet things were in the beginning! One was twenty years old, one dazzled both men and women, on every threshold all the fanfares rang out, one brought something new into the world, something completely unprecedented that the world undoubtedly was going to adore, as it was the reflection, the faithful picture, of primitive Idols.

What did it matter that one was extremely poor? Was it not just one more sign of greatness? One had, moreover, a satchel full of fruit that resembled the stars, gathered with both hands in the luminous forest, and one had faith in mankind.

But one day one noticed that people, disgusted with bread, loudly demanded potatoes; they wanted the soles of their feet rubbed with the fat of the small intestines of the Princes of Light – and this was the beginning of the agony that lasted thirty years.

monument to Villiers de l'Isle-Adam! to the author of *Isis*, *Tribulat Bonhomet*, *Contes cruels*, *The Future Eve*, *Axël* – everything he had written that was of the most bitter, most striking, most belting, most dog-whipping kind! and who spoke about it? Nobody.

It happened just recently that Villiers' work, having penetrated the soul of an intuitive sculptor – Frédéric Brou, the already celebrated artist of the bas-reliefs for Benjamin Franklin's monument – became concretized, solidified, petrified synthetically in him, to the point where Villiers himself who had wished to be cast in marble or bronze would have been unable to dictate anything different from the really extraordinary group statue printed on the first page of this small book.[3]

The erection of such a monument is, moreover, difficult to conceive of. Think about it – the group comprises, in reality, I do not say three people, but three figures. There is, as I have said, Glory, *stimulating* glory – such as Villiers could have understood it. She is called Tullia Fabriana, Claire Lenoir, Ellen, Morgane, Sara, Akédysséril; a *unique* woman, in both senses of the word. Then there is Villiers himself awakening and, finally, Death represented by that coffin, standing upright like a man, making a great effort to resist Glory!

---

[3]first page: on the first page of the original, but on the *cover* of this edition.

*
* *

Try to imagine the alarm, the panic felt by the multi-tudes on seeing that third figure standing upright in a public square, like a scaffold or a throne, like that Greek throne that poor Villiers felt he had a right to:

> *A throne, for him who dreams,*
> *A throne is rather dark these days!...*
> *It is made of four planks*
> *Absolutely like a coffin!*

The Bourgeois Man, the "Swan Slayer," as our poet referred to him, does not like it when some-one reminds him of the cemetery. He is not lyrical, him, he does not dream, he does not believe that one wakes up in tombs. His vile flesh which makes flow-ers fetid and which makes worms kick the bucket, he does not imagine it coming alive again. So the final end exasperates that reprobate, and everything that re-minds him of it fills his gob with maledictions and foam.

*
* *

It would be just fine and admirable however, and so noble, and how very just! if there were here and there in Montmartre or in the Luxembourg Garden – in this Paris so horribly sullied and disfigured by stupidity, but which is, all the same, still the old Paris of the elect – such a protestation of Poesy against Death!

But, once again, what fear and what fury! Jesus himself is called the Life, and it is for this reason that he will resuscitate, one day, all the dead. There will never be anything quite so frightening. For a great number of people, that will be, on the last step of the staircase of time, the first groaning of Eternal Terror.

While waiting, such an affirmation of the survival of a poet would be world-shattering. No one would be resuscitated after that, something that is infinitely probable, but there is also the chance for those who could have, for such a long time now, shown signs of living – to be horrified to death. In the case of Villiers de l'Isle-Adam primarily, the experiment is worth attempting.

**T**hink on it then. The central preoccupation, the umbilicus, of the singular poet who was the author of *The Future Eve* was – and this is something that must be completely intolerable to imbeciles – was his really unprecedented need for a restitution of woman. So rare a manner of being that it is almost impossible to speak about it without seeming to solicit a padded cell for oneself.

I wonder if you read that carefully. I have just written these words: *Restitution of Woman.*

It has nothing to do with a pleading, with a dithyrambic paranymph, with such and such fawning praise for the dangerous Sex. It has to do with a renewal of earthly Paradise, after the harsh winter of six thousand years. It has to do with rediscovering that famous Garden of Voluptuousness, the symbol and *accomplishment* of Woman, which all men gropingly search for throughout the centuries.

Being a poet and the particular poet that he was, Villiers had more need than another for a woman, for that *non plus ultra* of a Woman whom nobody can resist, were it God the Father himself, her whose eyebrow stokes the heart of Saints and of whom it was written that "She will laugh on the last day."

He had so fierce a need for her that after having sought her, for twenty years, among the phantoms of his dreams, he resolutely tried to create her, as a God would have done, with some dirt and saliva.

The Future Eve is the result of that Titanic effort, and it is almost a question to ask: was that Eve, prior to the catastrophe that destroyed her, was she capable of living. One could interrogate M. Thomas Alva Edison about it, whom Villiers extolled and glorified till the end of time.

In any case, she lived in him, in what a frothy life! and that is she whom I see pulling off the planks of his coffin!

*
* *

Yes, from *Isis* to *Axël*, he had a dream of the infinitely beautiful Woman, as strong and solid as the columns of heaven, as omniscient as He who presides over the Cherubim, a Woman who would be God! That was his personal and particular idea, his vision, rather, of the Holy Spirit who is that divine Third Person through which everything must be accomplished and which Woman symbolizes in a very mysterious way.

This preoccupation had, in him, something of the supernatural to it. A complete stranger, moreover, to Exegesis, to sacred Hermeneutics, and not possessing, like the Christian that he could have been and *thought he was*, a rigid rule, a *Credo,* that centuries could not bend, distorted by Hegelianism and ravaged by the most dangerous curiosities, at times incredibly devoid of equilibrium, he never understood the grandiose presentiment, I believe, that oppressed him for thirty or forty years.

*
* *

In vain, it appears, did that lofty poet receive all his gifts: Beauty, Genius, Nobility, absolute Courage, expansive and all-powerful Sympathy. His imaginative and lyrical faculties in permanent activity, and they remind one of those wandering stars in the Holy Bible,[4] but principally the archangelic promptitude of his epigrams, who does not remember them?

Eh, well! all that and more could not prevail against the inextirpable formulas of a German prig.[5] The blindness of that eagle was procured by the bedazzlement of this lantern! For his entire life, he sought his soul in the light of a sad philosophical blood-sausage mistaken for the true light. It is impossible to imagine a profounder misery.

*
* *

And nevertheless that soul that he so longed for, so sought after, that soul that he did not see the Blood of Christ flowing on, he recognized it as precious enough, for all that, to speak about it with greatness.

"She considered her soul too precious, in all the universe, to reveal it."

"Her soul hovered in her thoughts like an eagle in darkness."

---

[4]wandering stars: see Jude 1:13.

[5]German prig: Hegel.

"Of course, her brilliant friends and dancing partners had no idea that their compliments or words fell into her deep soul just like, in winter, the sounds of a bell tower from distant villages, carried by the nocturnal blasts of wind, penetrate the emptiness of space."

The woman referred to here is Tullia Fabriana in *Isis*, that is to say some female incarnation of Villiers' and who was endowed by him, since then, of all the marvels of his paradise.

"Men gifted with *intuitive incarnation*," he said, "put themselves in another person's shoes and look at themselves as if in the mirror... Behind the veil of what a man says, everything that is conveyed, evoked, or expressed is nothing but himself." This formula, horribly Hegelian, recurs constantly [throughout his work].

o not cast me aside. And to what end? I am unforgettable," said Sara, taking Axël in her arms. "*Do you realize what you*

are refusing? All the favors of other women are nothing compared to my cruelties! I am the darkest of virgins. I seem to recall angels having fallen for me. Alas! flowers and children have died in my shadow.

"Let yourself to be seduced! – I will teach you marvelous syllables that will intoxicate you like Oriental wines. I can put you asleep by caresses that kill. I know the secret of infinite pleasures and delicious cries, voluptuousnesses where all hope fails. Oh! to enshroud you in my whiteness, where you will leave your soul behind like a flower lost in the snow! To cover you in my hair where you will breathe the spirit of dead roses!... Cede. I will make you turn pale under bitter joys; I will have some clemency for you, when you are experiencing these tortures!... My kiss, it is as if you were drinking the sky! My breath is warmer than the first breezes of springtime on the savannas – more penetrating than the smoke of cassolettes burning in the seraglios of Cordova, more charged with forgetfulness than the perfumes coming from cedar planks nailed to trees by mages in the gardens of Bagdad in order to humiliate divine flowers.

"Look into my eyes and recognize the soul of beautiful nights, when you walked in the valleys and looked up at heaven; I am that exile on unknown stars whom you were looking for! I would give all the treasures in the world to be yours forever. Oh! to quit life without having to bathe your eyes in tears, those proud blue stars, those eyes of hope! oh! without having to make you shiver under the profound music of my loving voice! – Oh! the thought of it – it would be frightful, it would be impossible! To renounce this exceeds all my courage. Abandon yourself, say it, Axël – Axël!... And I will make you stammer on my lips the vows that give the greatest suffering – and all the dreams of your desire will pass into my eyes so as to multiply your kisses..."

*
* *

Akédysséril is another vision of the same creature, of the Woman one cannot forget, and for whom one dies as if before the Face of God.

"That snow-white girl of the solar race was of taller than most. The mauve purple headband, entwined with long diamonds and faded in battles, crowned, with its tall golden points, the pallor of her forehead. Her hair, floating down over her svelte and muscular back, blended its bluish shadows, over the golden fabric of her dress, with the bandelets of her diadem. Her traits were of an oppressive charm that, at first, inspired more agitation than love. Meanwhile, innumerable children, in the Habad, languished in silence for having seen her.

"A pale amber glow, infused in her flesh, enlivened the contours of her body: just like those transparencies whereby dawn, veiled by Himalayan heights, penetrates its whitenesses, as if from within.

"Below the horizontal immobility of her long eyelashes, two somber blue lights – within her languid Hindu eyelids, two magnificent eyes surcharged with dreams, dispensed around her a transformative magic on all the things of the earth and heaven. They saturated with unknown enchantments the fatal strangeness of that face whose beauty *could not be forgotten*.

"And the prominence of her haughty temples, the subtle oval of her cheeks, her cruel upturned nostrils that quivered in the perilous wind, her mouth gleaming with a touch of blood, her chin of a silent despoileratrix, the ever serious smile wherein her panther teeth gleamed, all that in its entirety, and veiled by dark distances, grew into the most magnificent of seductions when one had experienced the radiance of her starry eyes."

"very time you LOVE, you die an equal amount," the grumbling Hegel responds, and now look how all that gold dust is swept away.

What is remarkable here is the antagonism between the Christian island of Rhodes and the German philosopher. The child of knights would like to worship outside of himself, while the schoolboy of sauerkraut worships within himself. Oh! it's not easy to understand!

"You are only what you think: think of yourself then as eternal... You are your future creator. You are a God who does not feign to forget his complete essence only to realize the radiance of it. What you call the universe is nothing more than the result of that pretense which you hold the secret to. Recognize yourself! Talk yourself into Being! Extract yourself from the jail of the world, child of prisoners. Evade Becoming! Your 'truth' will be what you will have conceived: its essence is it not infinite like yourself!...

"You consider yourself *poor*, you who, with one look, can possess the world! You want also to *buy*, like humans, and to look over contracts, to push papers – to be SURE that you possess something! Thus you will not believe yourself master of a palace that you contemplate unless you become, by contract, the prisoner of its stones, the slave of its valets, the envy of its hosts rolling their empty eyes at you! Whereas instead you ought to be able to enter there and, before your presence alone and your sovereign expression, all the servants would come and obey you, and the so-called "master" of that same palace would tell them, while stammering, and bowing before you: – 'Address yourselves to him!'...

"Do you accept Light, Hope, and Life?"

That question is made, one after the other, to two young and gorgeous beings who are adored, by a delegation of Darknesses, Despair, and Death. "To live!" they responded, "the servants will do that for us," and they decide to die together on that oath of madness. I have never seen anything more afflicting than that complete disorder in so magnificent an intellectual Louvre.

*
* *

"I don't ask for better than to get down on my knees before my Creator, but on the condition that it be really before Him that I get down on my knees and not before the idea that I have of him. I ask merely to adore God, but I do not care to adore myself under that name, unbeknownst to myself. And it is difficult to recognize myself in him."

Dreadful power of malicious Hegelian stupidity that that haughty persifleur never could free himself from, even though warned about it by *his* familial tradition and nourished by four centuries of Christian milk.

"And yet, if only they were sincere, those philosophers!" he wrote, previously, in *Isis*. "But they aren't pleased unless they are throwing cold water on the peaceful hope of others. Every word contains a force, and as they speak, with little concern for the scandal contained in their words, *that scandal, being something, progresses through the crowds and across the centuries...*"

I have seen that man weep on remembering Our Lord Jesus Christ, from whom he could believe himself separated by forty abysses.

*

* *

Delights of the Imagination, voluptuousnesses of the Dream, who will know you like he knew you? By the example of all poets, Villiers de l'Isle-Adam contained in himself a kind of earthly Paradise. And it is for this reason that he needed the *Future Eve*, that book of a magician, splendid and desperate, totally incomprehensible for a generation that has completely forgotten about the Invisible and the Impalpable.

But what man, I wonder, was ever honored as much as Mr. Edison is, the hero – better yet, the protagonist – of that infinitely extraordinary book?...

I no longer wish to afflict myself by rehashing the excessive misfortune of that great artist imprisoned in a philosophical cottage and begging the beneficence of the stars for a moment's freedom.

The childishness of the hermetic harangues of Master Janus,[6] for instance, compared to those *Epistles* by Saint Paul out of which thunder issues, as Saint Jerome said, is enough to make a man sob.

What remains is this, that the most beautiful memory of the Human Race – the Virgin Bride of Paradise – has been fixed, for better or for worse, in a poem of fire and light, and that the glory of that marvel is a homage to the great American genius.

---

[6]Master Janus; a character in *Axël*.

I realize now that I have not yet spoken of the *hidden treasures,* and it is certainly not the smallest place of that luminous cavern that was Villiers' imagination.

Those who saw him often – friends or enemies, alas! – know that he openly spoke about a treasure or a mass of immobilized, unused treasures sleeping for generations in one-does-not-know-what ancestral crypt, and which he hoped to find one day, powerful lever by which he intended to stir up the world.

"Indifferent to the political concerns of this century and this country, to the passing forfeits of those who represent them, I linger behind when the evenings of solemn autumn set the treetops of the surrounding forests red with fire. Among the splendors of the dew, I walk alone under the vaults of the dark alleyways, like the Ancestor walked beneath the crypts of the scintillating cemetery! Instinctively, also, I avoid, I do know know why, the unlucky light of the moon and the harmful approach of humans. Yes, I avoid them, when I walk in this way together with my dreams!... For I feel *then* that I carry in my soul the reflection of the sterile riches of a great number of forgotten kings."

When the poor and dear poet was thinking of that, there was not a more disarmed man on earth. He went to bed, he wallowed in the delights of his hope; he would have subscribed to the short-term retaking of the island of Rhodes and of all the kingdoms or principalities of the Levant; he would have signed the death warrant for a hundred million Muslims and their withdrawal from Paradise! Just how deep that treasure was buried within him – he himself did not know.

*
* *

"The master faculty of the Artist," I wrote one day, while thinking of Villiers, "the Imagination, is naturally and passionately anarchic. It ignores instructions and rendezvous and burns like a solfatara. Creation is its prey, the Angels are its Vivandiers, and the Universe is its camp of choice. The infiniteness of space is its skylight in order to explore the totality of the centuries. It is the mother of the Alpha and the younger sister of the Omega, and the symbolic Serpent is its belt when it dresses up in formal attire only to think on God whom it is the profound mirror of.

"She assembles the clouds, better than Jupiter, thickly grouping them around herself as fancy takes her, and as she pleases she dissipates them instantly or makes them burst in deluge. The most unshakeable and heaviest masses leap and bound as soon as that Empress of Dreams gives them a sign.

"She is the providence and the curing of human passions. She perfumes impurities, disinfects elegances, gilds the teeth of crocodiles, repatriates the intoxication of perfect love in the oldest of hearts, finds marble veins in a flesh wrecked by syphilis, covers the most repugnant baldness by decorative caps, confers the sapidity of ambrosia to vomiting.

"All things diabolical and all things divine are contained within her because she was invested with the conservatorship of Art to which everything is necessary, and because she is forever, for its lost pupils, 'the Guardian Angel, the Muse, and the Madonna,' she before whom Baudelaire, in a poem of fatal beauty, recommended that one genuflect.

"Any capacity whatsoever – is it not laughable in the presence of that capriciousness of the Infinite, that straddling of Heaven? And those whom one calls great critics, when they are not always aberrant pedagogues, what could they possibly be if not just more drunkards of Fantasy, in search of their own bed to lie in in strange domiciles?"

nd now, it is to you whom I address myself, Thomas Alva Edison. Will you not do anything for the man who did so much for you?

If you are known in France for anything other than your inventions, "sorcerer of Menlo Park," it is because Villiers de l'Isle-Adam, blown away by what God had given you, had decided that it would be so.

Esteeming your work a cut above what is humanly possible, he thought that you had received gifts that made you a little more than a man, and that you ought to possess a soul similar to your genius. You would live for a thousand years, and you would change the sad face of the world where no man could do more for you than he did.

Be generous then for this great poet who heaped praise on you, and give magnificently. There are a small number of poor folk who want his glory just as he wanted yours, and we look for the means to realize the monument that would be necessary, the monument he deserves, the only monument that expresses his genius precisely, powerfully, pathetically, and forever, as he intended to express yours in a work that cannot die.

It is said in the Holy Bible that "No prophet is accepted in his own country."[7] Miraculously excepted from this harsh law, Mr. Edison, one hopes from you a grandiose act in favor of the magnanimous poet who experienced it in spades, when he glorified you

---

[7]"No prophet is accepted in his own country": Luke 4:24.

forever.

That would also be perhaps the secret to separating him once and for all, and definitively, from the banal multitude whom he so detested. He is, for seventeen years now, among the dead, that Immortal, that stubborn solitary, who was never able to find consolation for having been born among men.

"I drink to you," he wrote, "I drink to you, forest, giver of forgetfulness; moist grasses; wild roses that grow beneath the oaks, drunk on the dew that falls from their heavy foliage; to you, shores, where, in the evening, the saline odors of star-filled waves waft over them, and where you spread out, like me, magnificent and solitary."

Other Books by the Publisher

Fanchette's Pretty Little Foot by Restif de La Bretonne

Je M'Accuse... by Léon Bloy

My Hospitals & My Prisons by Paul Verlaine

Salvation Through the Jews by Léon Bloy

Words of a Demolitions Contractor by Léon Bloy

Cellulely by Paul Verlaine

Ecclesiastical Laurels by Jacques Rochette de la Morlière

Flowers of Bitumen by Émile Goudeau

Songs for Her & Odes in Her Honor by Paul Verlaine

On Huysmans' Tomb by Léon Bloy

Ten Years a Bohemian by Émile Goudeau

The Soul of Napoleon by Léon Bloy

Blood of the Poor by Léon Bloy

Joan of Arc and Germany by Léon Bloy

www.ingramcontent.com/pod-product-compliance
Lightning Source LLC
Chambersburg PA
CBHW020811130626
46554CB00006B/2387